Mastering the Art of

Public Speaking

In One Month

Mastering the Art of

Public Speaking

In One Month

Victor Mikah

Mastering the Art of Public Speaking in One Month

ISBN: 978-81-19524-34-1

First published in India in 2024 by Exceller Books,
An imprint of GE Group

Address: G1, Dream Apartment, Degree College Road, Belgharia, Kolkata, 700056, India

www.excellerbooks.com

Dedication

To everyone who has ever stood before an audience with trembling hands and a racing heart, yet found the courage to speak—this book is dedicated to you. May it serve as a guide and a beacon, helping you transform your fears into confidence and your words into powerful tools of connection and influence.

Acknowledgment

I would like to express my deepest gratitude to all those who have supported and encouraged me throughout this journey. To my family and friends, thank you for your unwavering belief in my abilities and for standing by me every step of the way. Special thanks to my mentors and colleagues, whose guidance and insights have been invaluable. Lastly, to everyone who struggles with public speaking and stage fright, this book is for you. My hope is that these pages provide you with the tools and inspiration to overcome your fears and become a confident speaker.

Table of Contents

Introduction

Public speaking is a skill that transcends professions, industries, and personal backgrounds. Whether you are a business executive presenting a strategy, a teacher explaining a complex topic, a community leader rallying support, or simply someone looking to articulate ideas more effectively, the ability to speak confidently and persuasively is invaluable. This book is designed to equip you with the tools, techniques, and confidence to become an effective public speaker, regardless of your starting point.

Public speaking is not just about delivering speeches; it is about communicating ideas, influencing decisions, and inspiring change. Public speaking plays a crucial role in different aspects of life.

In the workplace, public speaking skills are essential for presenting ideas clearly and confidently. They enhance your ability to lead meetings, pitch proposals, and represent your organisation.

Effective communicators are often seen as leaders and are more likely to advance in their careers.

Public speaking boosts self-confidence and self-awareness. It encourages you to articulate your thoughts and stand by your ideas.

It also improves critical thinking and quick decision-making skills as you learn to respond to audience reactions and questions on the spot.

Whether you're advocating for a course, campaigning for a public office, or volunteering in community activities, the ability to speak persuasively can help you mobilise support and drive action.

Public speakers often become influential figures in their communities, shaping public opinion and leading social change.

This book is structured to take you on a comprehensive journey from understanding the fundamentals of public speaking to mastering advanced techniques.

Embarking on the journey to become an effective public speaker can be both exciting and challenging. Remember, every great speaker started somewhere. This book is your companion, providing you with the knowledge, tools, and encouragement to grow and succeed. By committing to the process and applying the lessons learned, you can transform your public speaking abilities and unlock new opportunities in your personal and professional life.

Chapter I

Understanding Public Speaking

Definition and History of Public Speaking

What is Public Speaking?

Public speaking is the process of communicating information to an audience. It is typically done before a live audience in a structured, deliberate manner intended to inform, influence, or entertain the listeners. Public speaking encompasses a wide range of speaking engagements, from formal presentations and speeches to informal talks and discussions.

The Evolution of Public Speaking

Public speaking has been an essential skill throughout human history. Its origins can be traced back to ancient civilizations, where it was used for political, social, and educational purposes.

1. Ancient Greece and Rome:

- The art of public speaking, or rhetoric, was highly valued in ancient Greece. Notable figures like Aristotle, Plato, and Socrates contributed significantly to its development. Aristotle's "Rhetoric" is a seminal work that outlines the principles of effective speaking.

- In ancient Rome, public speaking was a critical skill for politicians and lawyers. Cicero and Quintilian were among the most renowned Roman orators who left a lasting impact on the principles of rhetoric.

2. Middle Ages and Renaissance:

- During the Middle Ages, the focus shifted slightly to preaching and religious discourse, with notable speakers like Thomas Aquinas.
- The Renaissance brought a renewed interest in classical rhetoric, with scholars such as Erasmus and Thomas More emphasizing the importance of effective communication.

3. Modern Era:

The 19th and 20th centuries saw the rise of notable public speakers who used the platform for political and social change. Figures like Abraham Lincoln, Winston Churchill, and Martin Luther King Jr. demonstrated the power of public speaking to influence public opinion and drive societal progress.

The Role of Public Speaking in Different Cultures

Public speaking is a universal form of communication, but its practice and importance vary across cultures.

Western Cultures:

- In Western cultures, public speaking is often associated with individual expression and leadership. It is a critical skill in politics, business, and education.
- Western rhetoric focuses on logical argumentation, persuasive techniques, and the clear articulation of ideas.

Eastern Cultures:

- In many Eastern cultures, public speaking emphasizes harmony, respect, and collective well-being. The style may be more indirect, with a focus on consensus and group harmony.
- Storytelling, proverbs, and metaphors are commonly used to convey messages in an engaging and culturally resonant manner.

African Cultures:

- African public speaking traditions often involve communal participation, with a strong emphasis on oral storytelling and performance.

- Speakers use rhythm, music, and call-and-response techniques to engage the audience and reinforce the communal experience.

Indigenous Cultures:

- Indigenous public speaking practices often incorporate spiritual and ritualistic elements, with a focus on preserving cultural heritage and oral traditions.
- Elders and community leaders play a crucial role in public speaking, serving as custodians of wisdom and cultural knowledge.

Famous Public Speakers and Their Impact

Throughout history, many individuals have distinguished themselves as powerful public speakers. Their speeches have left an indelible mark on society and continue to inspire future generations.

Ancient Times:

- Demosthenes: A prominent Greek orator known for his powerful and persuasive speeches. His "Philippics" against Philip II of Macedon are famous examples of his oratory skills.
- Cicero: A Roman statesman and orator who mastered the art of rhetoric. His speeches, such as "In Catilinam," showcase his ability to persuade and mobilize public opinion.

Modern Era:

- Abraham Lincoln: The 16th President of the United States, known for his eloquence and ability to connect with his audience. The "Gettysburg Address" remains one of the most iconic speeches in American history.

- Winston Churchill: The British Prime Minister during World War II, renowned for his stirring speeches that bolstered British morale. His speech "We Shall Fight on the Beaches" is a testament to his rhetorical prowess.

- Martin Luther King Jr.: A leader of the American civil rights movement. His speeches, such as "I Have a Dream," exemplify the power of public speaking to inspire and effect social change.

- Nelson Mandela: The anti-apartheid revolutionary and former President of South Africa, Mandela's speeches emphasized reconciliation and the fight for justice, profoundly impacting global perspectives on equality and freedom.

Contemporary Speakers:

- Barack Obama: The 44th President of the United States, known for his articulate and inspiring speeches. His ability to connect with diverse audiences has made him one of the most influential speakers of the 21st century.

- Malala Yousafzai: The youngest-ever Nobel Prize laureate, Malala's speeches advocate for girls' education and human rights, highlighting her courage and resilience.
- Greta Thunberg: The young climate activist whose speeches have galvanized global action on climate change. Her straightforward and passionate delivery has made her a powerful voice for environmental issues.

Understanding the history and cultural significance of public speaking provides a foundation for appreciating its role in contemporary society. From ancient Greece to modern-day platforms, public speaking continues to be a vital skill for influencing, inspiring, and effecting change.

By learning from past masters and recognizing the diverse traditions across cultures, aspiring public speakers can develop a deeper appreciation and mastery of this timeless art.

Chapter 2

Overcoming Fear and Building Confidence

Common Fears and Anxieties Associated with Public Speaking

Understanding Glossophobia

Glossophobia, or the fear of public speaking, is one of the most common phobias, affecting an estimated 75% of people. This fear can manifest in various ways, including physical symptoms such as sweating, trembling, a racing heart, and dry mouth, as well as psychological symptoms like intense anxiety and fear of judgement.

Sources of Public Speaking Anxiety

1. Fear of Failure:

The fear of making mistakes or failing to deliver a perfect speech can paralyze speakers. This often stems from high self-expectations and the pressure to perform flawlessly.

2. Fear of Judgment:

The concern that the audience will judge or criticize your performance can lead to anxiety. This fear is heightened when speaking in front of authority figures, peers, or large groups.

3. Lack of Experience:

Inexperience in public speaking can cause uncertainty and nervousness. The unfamiliarity with the process and lack of practice contribute to anxiety.

4. Negative Past Experiences:

Previous experiences of public speaking that did not go well can lead to a lasting fear. These memories can create a mental block, making future attempts more daunting.

Psychological Techniques to Overcome Fear

1. Cognitive Behavioral Techniques (CBTs):

CBTs focus on changing negative thought patterns and behaviours. Techniques include identifying irrational fears, challenging negative thoughts, and gradually exposing oneself to the feared situation.

2. Visualisation:

Visualization involves imagining yourself delivering a successful speech. By picturing a positive outcome, you can reduce anxiety and build confidence.

3. Positive Affirmations:

Repeating positive affirmations can help reframe your mindset. Phrases like "I am a confident and effective speaker" can reinforce a positive self-image.

4. Mindfulness and Meditation:

Practising mindfulness and meditation can help calm the mind and reduce anxiety. Techniques such as deep breathing and focused attention can ground you in the present moment.

Practical Exercises to Build Confidence

1. Gradual Exposure:

Start by speaking in low-stakes situations and gradually increase the level of difficulty. Begin with small groups of friends or family and work your way up to larger audiences.

2. Role-Playing:

Practise your speech with a trusted friend or colleague who can provide constructive feedback. Role-playing different scenarios can help you prepare for various audience reactions.

3. Public Speaking Clubs:

Joining organizations like Toastmasters provides a supportive environment for practising and improving your public speaking skills. Regular participation helps build confidence through experience and feedback.

4. Breathing Exercises:

Deep breathing exercises can help calm your nerves before speaking. Practise inhaling deeply through your nose, holding for a few seconds, and exhaling slowly through your mouth.

5. Voice and Body Warm-Ups:

Physical warm-ups, such as stretching and shaking out your limbs, can release tension. Vocal warm-ups, like humming and tongue twisters, can improve your voice quality and reduce nervousness.

Real-Life Stories of Overcoming Public Speaking Anxiety

Story 1: Abraham Lincoln

Abraham Lincoln, one of America's greatest orators, struggled with public speaking early in his career. He faced criticism for his high-pitched voice and awkward mannerisms. However, Lincoln persevered, practising his speeches rigorously and seeking feedback. Over time, he developed a commanding presence and delivered some of the most memorable speeches in history, including the Gettysburg Address.

Story 2: Warren Buffett

Warren Buffett, one of the most successful investors in the world, experienced intense fear of public speaking in his youth. He avoided speaking engagements and felt physically ill at the thought of presenting. Determined to overcome this fear, Buffett enrolled in a Dale Carnegie public speaking course. Through practice and persistence, he conquered his anxiety and now confidently addresses shareholders and audiences worldwide.

Story 3: Oprah Winfrey

Oprah Winfrey, a media mogul and influential public speaker, faced significant anxiety early in her career. Despite her natural charisma, she feared public failure and judgement. Winfrey worked tirelessly to hone her speaking skills, using visualization and positive affirmations to build confidence. Today, she is celebrated for her powerful and engaging speeches.

Overcoming the fear of public speaking is a journey that requires time, effort, and persistence. By understanding the root causes of your anxiety, employing psychological techniques, and engaging in practical exercises, you can gradually build confidence and become a more effective speaker. Remember, even the greatest orators started somewhere. With determination and practice, you, too, can conquer your fears and harness the power of public speaking to influence, inspire, and achieve your goals.

This chapter provides comprehensive strategies for overcoming fear and building confidence, combining psychological insights with practical exercises and inspirational stories.

Chapter 3

Knowing Your Audience

Importance of Understanding Your Audience

Why Audience Analysis Matters

Understanding your audience is crucial for crafting a message that resonates and engages effectively. When you know who you are speaking to, you can tailor your content, delivery style, and interaction methods to meet their needs and expectations. This alignment increases the likelihood of achieving your speech's goals, whether to inform, persuade, or entertain.

1. Connection and Engagement:

- Analyzing your audience helps you create a connection, making your speech more engaging and impactful.
- It enables you to address their interests, concerns, and motivations directly.

2. Relevance and Clarity:

- Tailoring your message to your audience ensures it is relevant and clear, avoiding confusion and disinterest.
- Understanding their knowledge level allows you to provide the appropriate amount of background information.

3. Effective Persuasion:

- Knowing your audience's values and beliefs helps construct persuasive arguments that are more likely to influence them.
- It enables you to anticipate objections and address them proactively.

Techniques for Audience Analysis

1. Demographic Analysis:

- Collect information on demographic factors such as age, gender, education level, occupation, cultural background, and socio-economic status.
- This data helps you understand the general characteristics and preferences of your audience.

2. Psychographic Analysis:

- Explore the audience's attitudes, values, interests, and lifestyles. This deeper insight helps you tailor your speech's emotional and psychological appeal.

- Consider factors like political beliefs, religious affiliations, and personal motivations.

3. Situational Analysis:

- Analyze the context of your speech, including the occasion, location, and time of day. The situation can significantly influence the audience's expectations and receptiveness.
- Consider the size of the audience and the physical setting to adjust your delivery style accordingly.

4. Audience Knowledge and Experience:

- Assess the audience's prior knowledge of the topic to determine the level of detail and complexity needed.
- Consider their experience and familiarity with similar content to avoid redundancy and keep them engaged.

5. Direct Methods:

- Conduct surveys or questionnaires to gather specific information about your audience's interests and expectations.
- Use interviews or focus groups for more in-depth understanding.

6. Indirect Methods:

- Observe the audience's behaviour and interactions in similar settings to infer their preferences and expectations.
- Analyse social media profiles and online behaviour for additional insights.

Adapting Your Message to Different Types of Audiences

1. Expert vs. Novice Audiences:

- For expert audiences, delve into detailed and technical aspects, using industry jargon appropriately.
- For novice audiences, simplify complex concepts and provide clear explanations and analogies.

2. Homogeneous vs. Heterogeneous Audiences:

- Homogeneous audiences share common characteristics, making it easier to tailor a focused message.
- Heterogeneous audiences require a more balanced approach, addressing diverse interests and backgrounds.

3. Supportive vs. Hostile Audiences:

- With supportive audiences, reinforce their beliefs and provide additional validation for their viewpoints.
- With hostile audiences, approach with empathy, acknowledge their concerns and present your arguments respectfully and logically.

4. Cultural Differences:

- Be aware of cultural norms and values, adapting your speech to respect and resonate with diverse cultural backgrounds.
- Use culturally relevant examples and avoid language or gestures that may be misinterpreted or offensive.

Engaging with Diverse Audiences

1. Inclusive Language:

- Use language that is inclusive and avoids alienating any group within your audience.
- Be mindful of pronouns, terminology, and expressions that respect diversity.

2. Interactive Techniques:

- Engage the audience through questions, polls, and interactive activities that encourage participation.

- Use storytelling and relatable anecdotes to bridge gaps between diverse audience members.

3. Visual and Aural Aids:

- Incorporate visual aids like slides, videos, and infographics to illustrate points and maintain interest.
- Use a variety of vocal tones and pacing to keep the audience engaged and emphasize key points.

4. Feedback and Adaptation:

- Pay attention to non-verbal cues from the audience, such as body language and facial expressions, to gauge their engagement and understanding.
- Be prepared to adapt your delivery in real time based on audience reactions and feedback.

Understanding your audience is a foundational aspect of effective public speaking. By conducting a thorough audience analysis and adapting your message to their needs, you can create a more engaging, relevant, and impactful speech. Remember, the key to successful communication lies in connecting with your audience on their terms, addressing their concerns, and delivering your message in a way that resonates with them. By mastering the art of audience analysis and adaptation, you can enhance your public speaking effectiveness and achieve your communication goals.

This chapter provides a detailed exploration of the importance of audience analysis, techniques for understanding your audience, and strategies for engaging different types of audiences.

Chapter 4
Crafting Your Message

Identifying Your Purpose and Key Message

Clarifying Your Purpose

Before you begin crafting your speech, it is crucial to identify the primary purpose of your message. Your purpose will guide the content, structure, and tone of your speech. Generally, public speaking purposes fall into three main categories:

1. To Inform:

The goal is to educate the audience about a specific topic, providing facts, data, and insights.

Examples: lectures, business presentations, and technical briefings

2. To Persuade:

The aim is to convince the audience to adopt a particular viewpoint or take a specific action.

Examples: political speeches, sales pitches, and motivational talks

3. To Entertain:

The focus is on engaging and entertaining the audience, often through humour, storytelling, or dramatic performances.

Examples: after-dinner speeches, stand-up comedy, and keynote addresses at celebratory events

Defining Your Key Message

Once you have identified your purpose, distil your message into a clear, concise key statement. This statement encapsulates the main idea you want your audience to remember and take away. It should be:

- Clear: Easily understood without ambiguity
- Concise: Short and to the point, avoiding unnecessary details
- Compelling: Interesting and engaging to capture the audience's attention

Example: If your purpose is to persuade people to adopt eco-friendly practices, your key message might be, "Adopting simple eco-friendly habits can significantly reduce our environmental impact and create a sustainable future for generations to come."

Structuring Your Speech: Introduction, Body, Conclusion

The Introduction

The introduction sets the stage for your speech, grabbing the audience's attention and establishing the context. A strong introduction typically includes the following:

1. Attention-Grabber:

- Start with a hook to capture interest. This could be a startling fact, a relevant quote, a rhetorical question, a short anecdote, or a joke (if appropriate).

2. Purpose and Relevance:

- Clearly state the purpose of your speech and explain why it is relevant to your audience.

3. Preview of Main Points:

- Provide a brief overview of the main points you will cover, setting expectations for the audience.

Example: "Imagine a world where every household saves hundreds of dollars on energy bills while also saving the planet. Today, I'm going to share with you how adopting simple eco-friendly habits can help achieve this."

The Body

The body of your speech contains the main content and arguments. It should be organised logically, with clear transitions between points. Common organisational patterns include:

1. Chronological Order:

- Present information in the order in which it occurred or should occur. This is useful for historical topics or process explanations.

2. Topical Order:

- Divide your speech into key topics or themes. This works well for informative speeches covering different aspects of a subject.

3. Problem-Solution Order:

- Present a problem, followed by potential solutions. This is effective for persuasive speeches.

4. Cause-Effect Order:

- Discuss the causes of a problem and its effects. This approach is useful for analytical speeches.

Each main point should be supported by evidence, such as statistics, quotes, examples, and anecdotes. Ensure that each point relates to your key message.

Example:

1. Main Point 1: The Environmental Impact of Everyday Habits

- Discuss the carbon footprint of common household activities.
- Provide statistics on energy consumption and waste production.

2. Main Point 2: Simple Eco-Friendly Practices

- Explain practical steps like reducing water usage, recycling, and using energy-efficient appliances.
- Share success stories and examples from individuals or communities.

3. Main Point 3: Long-Term Benefits of Eco-Friendly Habits

- Highlight the financial savings and health benefits.
- Discuss the broader impact on the environment and future generations.

The Conclusion

The conclusion reinforces your key message and leaves a lasting impression. It typically includes:

1. Summary of Main Points:

- Recap the key points you covered in the body of your speech.

2. Restate the Key Message:

- Emphasise your main idea one last time to ensure it sticks with the audience.

3. Call to Action:

- If appropriate, encourage your audience to take specific action based on your speech.

4. Closing Remark:

- End with a memorable closing remark, such as a powerful quote, a final thought, or a call to reflect.

Example: "By adopting simple eco-friendly habits, we can significantly reduce our environmental impact, save money, and create a sustainable future. Let's start today and make a difference for tomorrow."

The Power of Storytelling in Public Speaking

Why Stories Matter

Stories are a powerful tool in public speaking because they:

- Engage Emotionally: Stories tap into the audience's emotions, making your message more relatable and memorable.
- Illustrate Points: They provide concrete examples that illustrate abstract ideas or complex concepts.
- Enhance Retention: People are more likely to remember stories than facts and figures alone.

Elements of a Good Story

A compelling story typically includes:

1. Characters:

- Introduce relatable characters that the audience can connect with. They can be real or fictional, depending on your speech.

2. Conflict:

- Present a challenge or conflict that the characters face. This creates tension and keeps the audience interested.

3. Resolution:

- Show how the conflict is resolved. This provides closure and reinforces your key message.

4. Moral or Lesson:

- Highlight the moral or lesson of the story, tying it back to your main point.

    Example: "When John, a single father, started implementing eco-friendly practices in his home, he not only reduced his utility bills but also inspired his neighbours to do the same. Together, their community saw a 20% decrease in energy consumption within a year. John's story shows that small changes can lead to big impacts."

Using Evidence and Examples Effectively

Types of Evidence

1. Statistics:
- Use data to support your points. Ensure the statistics are from reliable sources and relevant to your message.

2. Quotes:
- Incorporate quotes from experts, influential figures, or reputable publications to add credibility.

3. Examples:
- Provide specific examples that illustrate your points. These can be real-life cases, hypothetical scenarios, or personal anecdotes.

4. Analogies and Comparisons:
Use analogies and comparisons to make complex ideas more understandable and relatable.

Tips for Using Evidence

1. Be Selective:
- Choose the most relevant and compelling evidence to support your points. Avoid overwhelming your audience with too much data.

2. Explain Clearly:

- Always explain the significance of your evidence. Don't assume the audience will make the connections on their own.

3. Integrate Smoothly:

- Seamlessly integrate evidence into your speech rather than presenting it in a disjointed manner. Use transitions to connect evidence to your main points.

4. Cite Sources:

- Acknowledge your sources to maintain credibility. Mentioning reputable sources enhances the trustworthiness of your information.

Example: "According to the Environmental Protection Agency, the average household can save up to $150 annually by using energy-efficient appliances. This statistic, supported by numerous studies, highlights the financial benefits of adopting eco-friendly habits."

Crafting your message is a crucial step in public speaking that involves defining your purpose, structuring your speech effectively, and using storytelling and evidence to engage your audience. By following these guidelines, you can create a compelling and memorable speech that resonates with your audience and achieves your communication goals. Remember, a well-crafted message is the foundation of successful public speaking.

This chapter provides detailed guidance on crafting a speech, from identifying your purpose to effectively using storytelling and evidence, ensuring you deliver a powerful and engaging message.

Chapter 5
Developing Your Speaking Style

Finding Your Unique Voice and Style

The Importance of Authenticity
Authenticity in public speaking means presenting yourself in a genuine manner. Audiences can quickly detect when a speaker is being insincere or trying to mimic someone else. Being authentic helps build trust and makes your message more relatable and convincing.

1. Understanding Yourself:
- Reflect on your personality, values, and experiences. Your unique perspective is what sets you apart from other speakers.
- Identify your strengths and weaknesses as a speaker. Play to your strengths while working on areas that need improvement.

2. Consistency:
- Ensure your body language, tone of voice, and content are aligned. Consistency in these areas reinforces your authenticity.

- Stay true to your message and beliefs. Avoid saying what you think the audience wants to hear if it conflicts with your values.

3. Personal Stories and Anecdotes:

- Share personal stories that illustrate your points. This adds a personal touch and makes your message more compelling.
- Use anecdotes that reflect your experiences and values. This not only supports your authenticity but also helps the audience connect with you.

Developing Your Unique Style

Your speaking style is a combination of your delivery, language, and overall approach to communication. Developing a unique style involves finding what feels natural to you while engaging your audience effectively.

1. Experiment and Practice:

- Experiment with different speaking styles and techniques to see what works best for you.
- Practise regularly to refine your style and build confidence.

2. Feedback:

- Seek feedback from trusted peers, mentors, or public speaking groups. Constructive criticism helps you identify areas for improvement.

- Analyse feedback to understand what resonates with your audience and what doesn't.

3. Observation:

- Watch and learn from other speakers. Observe how they engage their audience, use body language, and vary their tone.
- Incorporate elements that you find effective while staying true to your style.

Enhancing Clarity and Conciseness

Clarity in Communication

Clarity ensures your audience understands your message without confusion. Clear communication involves using simple language, structured ideas, and avoiding jargon unless it is appropriate for the audience.

1. Simple Language:

- Use straightforward language that is easy to understand. Avoid complex words and technical jargon unless your audience is familiar with them.
- Aim for short sentences that convey your message effectively.

2. Structured Ideas:

- Organise your speech logically. Use clear headings, bullet points, and transitions to guide your audience through your ideas.
- Break down complex ideas into smaller, manageable parts. Use examples and analogies to make abstract concepts more tangible.

3. Repetition for Emphasis:

- Repeat key points to reinforce your message. This helps the audience retain important information.
- Use different phrasing or examples to restate key points without sounding redundant.

Conciseness in Communication

Conciseness means expressing your ideas without unnecessary words or details. A concise speech is more engaging and easier for the audience to follow.

1. Edit Ruthlessly:

- Review your speech and remove any redundant or irrelevant information. Focus on the essential points that support your key message.
- Aim for brevity without sacrificing clarity. Each sentence should add value to your overall message.

2. Avoid Fillers:

- Minimise the use of filler words such as "um," "like," and "you know." These can distract from your message and make you appear less confident.
- Practise speaking slowly and pausing when necessary. This gives you time to think and reduces the need for fillers.

3. Practise Precision:

- Choose words that precisely convey your meaning. Be specific rather than vague in your descriptions and explanations.
- Use active voice and strong verbs to make your speech more dynamic and direct.

Adding Emotional Appeal and Humor

Emotional Appeal

Emotional appeal involves connecting with your audience on an emotional level. This can make your speech more persuasive and memorable.

1. Identify Emotions:

- Determine the emotions you want to evoke in your audience. This could be excitement, empathy, motivation, or urgency.

- Use stories, examples, and anecdotes that trigger these emotions. Personal experiences and real-life examples are particularly effective.

2. Expressive Delivery:

- Use your tone of voice, facial expressions, and body language to convey emotions. A passionate delivery can amplify the emotional impact of your message.
- Match your delivery style to the emotions you want to evoke. For example, use a calm and soothing tone for a compassionate message or an energetic and enthusiastic tone for a motivational speech.

3. Empathy and Connection:

- Show empathy towards your audience's feelings and experiences. Acknowledge their emotions and perspectives.
- Create a sense of connection by sharing your own emotions and vulnerabilities. This makes you more relatable and human.

Incorporating Humour

Humour can make your speech more enjoyable and engaging, but it should be used appropriately and sparingly.

1. Know Your Audience:

- Understand the type of humour that resonates with your audience. Avoid jokes that could be offensive or misinterpreted.
- Tailor your humour to the context and setting of your speech. What works in a casual setting may not be appropriate in a formal one.

2. Natural Humour:

- Use humour that feels natural to you. Forced jokes can come across as inauthentic and awkward.
- Share funny anecdotes or observations that relate to your message. Personal stories can be particularly effective.

3. Timing and Pacing:

- Timing is crucial for humour. Pause after delivering a punch line to give the audience time to react.
- Avoid overloading your speech with jokes. Use humour strategically to enhance your message rather than overshadow it.

Balancing Content with Delivery

Content

Content refers to the substance of your speech. High-quality content is well-researched, relevant, and tailored to your audience.

1. Research and Preparation:

- Thoroughly research your topic to provide accurate and valuable information. Use credible sources to support your points.
- Prepare your speech in advance, organising your ideas logically and coherently.

2. Tailoring to Audience:

- Adapt your content to the interests and needs of your audience. Focus on what matters to them and address their concerns.
- Use examples and references that your audience can relate to.

Delivery

Delivery refers to how you present your content. Effective delivery involves clear articulation, appropriate pacing, and engaging body language.

1. Vocal Variety:

- Use changes in pitch, volume, and pace to maintain interest and emphasise key points.
- Avoid a monotone delivery, which can make your speech dull and difficult to follow.

2. Body Language:

- Use gestures, facial expressions, and movement to reinforce your message. Your body language should complement your words.
- Maintain eye contact with your audience to build connections and convey confidence.

3. Practise:

- Practise your delivery repeatedly to become comfortable with your material and delivery style.
- Record yourself to identify areas for improvement and practise in front of others for feedback.

Developing your speaking style is a dynamic and ongoing process. By finding your unique voice, enhancing clarity and conciseness, adding emotional appeal and humor, and balancing content with delivery, you can become a more effective and engaging speaker. Remember, authenticity and practice are key to refining your style and making a lasting impact on your audience. Embrace your individuality and let it shine through in your speeches, making each presentation a memorable and impactful experience.

This chapter provides detailed guidance on developing a unique speaking style, enhancing clarity and conciseness, incorporating emotional appeal and humour, and balancing content with delivery.

Chapter 6

Using Visual Aids Effectively

The Role of Visual Aids in Public Speaking

Enhancing Understanding

Visual aids play a critical role in public speaking by making complex information more accessible and understandable. They help illustrate points, clarify concepts, and keep the audience engaged.

1. Simplifying Complex Information:

- Visual aids can break down complex data or processes into simpler, more digestible parts.
- Diagrams, charts, and graphs can visually represent information that might be difficult to explain verbally.

2. Improving Retention:

- People tend to remember visual information better than text alone. Visual aids can reinforce key points and help the audience retain information.
- Using visuals alongside verbal explanations can enhance memory retention through dual coding,

where the brain processes both visual and verbal information.

3. Engaging the Audience:

- Visual aids can capture and hold the audience's attention, making your presentation more dynamic and interesting.
- They provide variety and break the monotony of continuous speech, making the overall experience more engaging.

Types of Visual Aids

1. Slides (PowerPoint, Keynote):

- Slides can include text, images, charts, and multimedia elements. They are versatile and widely used in presentations.
- Use slides to highlight key points, show visuals, and present data in a clear and structured way.

2. Charts and Graphs:

- Charts (bar, pie, line) and graphs are effective for presenting statistical data and trends.
- They provide a visual representation of data, making it easier for the audience to grasp and compare information.

3. Images and Photos:

- High-quality images and photos can illustrate points, evoke emotions, and create a visual context for your message.
- Use relevant and impactful images to enhance storytelling and emphasize key points.

4. Videos and Animations:

- Videos and animations can demonstrate processes, show real-life examples, and add dynamic elements to your presentation.
- Ensure that multimedia elements are high-quality and directly related to your message.

5. Props and Models:

- Physical objects, models, or prototypes can provide tangible examples and hands-on demonstrations.
- Use props to create a more interactive and memorable experience for your audience.

6. Hand-outs:

- Hand-outs can provide detailed information, summaries, or additional resources that the audience can take with them.
- Use hand-outs to complement your presentation and provide a reference for later review.

Designing Effective Visual Aids

Principles of Good Design

1. Simplicity:

- Keep visual aids simple and uncluttered. Focus on key points and avoid overloading slides with too much information.
- Use minimal text and highlight essential information with bullet points or keywords.

2. Consistency:

- Maintain a consistent design throughout your presentation. Use the same fonts, colours, and layout for all slides.
- Consistency in design creates a cohesive and professional look.

3. Readability:

- Ensure that the text is large enough to be read easily from a distance. Use clear and legible fonts.
- Avoid using too many different fonts, and stick to a maximum of two or three.

4. Contrast:

- Use contrasting colours for text and background to ensure readability. Dark text on a light background or light text on a dark background works well.

- Use colour strategically to highlight important points and create visual interest.

5. Alignment and Balance:

- Align elements properly to create a clean and organized look. Use grids or guides to ensure alignment.
- Balance visuals on the slide to avoid clutter and maintain a pleasing aesthetic.

Using Color and Fonts Effectively

1. Color Psychology:

- Understand the psychological impact of colours. Use colours that match the tone and purpose of your presentation.
- For example, blue can evoke trust and professionalism, while red can create a sense of urgency or importance.

2. Font Choice:

- Choose fonts that are easy to read and professional. Sans-serif fonts like Arial or Helvetica are commonly used for presentations.
- Avoid overly decorative fonts that can be difficult to read and distract from your message.

3. Colour Schemes:

- Use a consistent colour scheme throughout your presentation. Limit your palette to a few complementary colours.
- Use bold colours for headings and key points and more subdued colours for background elements.

Integrating Visuals Seamlessly into Your Presentation

1. Relevance:

- Ensure that all visual aids are directly related to your content. Avoid using visuals that do not add value to your message.
- Each visual should have a clear purpose and support your key points.

2. Timing and Placement:

- Introduce visual aids at the right moment to reinforce your message. Do not show visuals too early or leave them on the screen too long.
- Place visuals where they naturally fit within your speech, enhancing the flow of your presentation.

3. Smooth Transitions:

- Use smooth transitions between slides and visual elements. Avoid jarring effects that can distract the audience.

- Practise using transitions to ensure they enhance rather than hinder your delivery.

Tips for Using Visual Aids during Your Speech

Practice and Familiarity

1. Rehearse with Visual Aids:
- Practise your speech with the visual aids you plan to use. This helps you become comfortable with the timing and integration of visuals.
- Familiarise yourself with the technical aspects of your presentation tools to avoid technical glitches.

2. Backup Plans:
- Prepare for potential technical issues by having backup options, such as printed copies of your slides or alternative devices.
- Test all equipment and visual aids before your presentation to ensure everything works smoothly.

Engagement and Interaction

1. Refer to Visuals Naturally:
- Incorporate visual aids naturally into your speech. Refer to them when appropriate and use them to illustrate your points.

- Avoid reading directly from your slides. Instead, use visuals as a supplement to your spoken words.

2. Engage the Audience:

- Encourage the audience to look at the visual aids by directing their attention to specific elements.
- Ask questions or invite comments related to the visuals to foster interaction and engagement.

3. Maintain Eye Contact:

- While using visual aids, maintain eye contact with your audience. Do not turn your back to the audience or focus solely on the screen.
- Glance at the visual aids briefly to refer to them, and then return your focus to the audience.

Clarity and Emphasis

1. Explain Visuals Clearly:

- Provide clear explanations of what is shown in the visual aids. Do not assume the audience will interpret them correctly on their own.
- Highlight key elements of the visuals and explain their significance.

2. Use Pointers or Gestures:

- Use pointers, laser pointers, or gestures to draw attention to specific parts of the visual aids.

- Ensure your gestures are clear and deliberate to guide the audience's focus.

Using visual aids effectively can greatly enhance your public speaking by making your message clearer, more engaging, and easier to remember. By designing visually appealing and relevant aids, integrating them seamlessly into your presentation, and using them confidently during your speech, you can create a more impactful and professional presentation. Remember, visual aids should complement and reinforce your message, not overshadow it. With practice and thoughtful design, visual aids can become a powerful tool in your public speaking arsenal.

This chapter provides detailed guidance on the role of visual aids, designing effective visuals, integrating them into your presentation, and tips for using them during your speech to enhance clarity, engagement, and overall impact.

Chapter 7

Overcoming Nervousness and Building Confidence

Understanding the Causes of Nervousness

The Physiology of Nervousness

Nervousness before public speaking is a common experience, often driven by physiological responses to stress. Understanding these responses can help you manage them effectively.

1. Fight-or-Flight Response:
- The fight-or-flight response is an automatic reaction to perceived threats, triggering physical symptoms such as increased heart rate, sweating, and shallow breathing.
- Recognizing this response as a natural part of your body's defence mechanism can help you accept and manage it.

2. Adrenaline Surge:
- When faced with the stress of public speaking, your body releases adrenaline, which prepares you to

react quickly. This can cause jitteriness and heightened alertness.

- Channelling this energy positively can enhance your performance rather than hinder it.

3. Physical Symptoms:

- Common physical symptoms of nervousness include dry mouth, trembling, and a shaky voice.
- Awareness of these symptoms allows you to develop strategies to minimize their impact.

Psychological Factors

1. Fear of Judgment:

- The fear of being judged or criticized by the audience is a major source of anxiety for many speakers.
- Reminding yourself that the audience is generally supportive and understanding can help alleviate this fear.

2. Perfectionism:

- The desire to deliver a flawless performance can create immense pressure, leading to increased nervousness.
- Accepting that mistakes are a natural part of public speaking and that they can be recovered from can reduce anxiety.

3. Lack of Experience:

- Inexperience in public speaking can contribute to nervousness, as unfamiliar situations often trigger anxiety.
- Gaining experience through practice and smaller speaking opportunities can build confidence over time.

Techniques for Managing Nervousness

Preparation and Practice

1. Thorough Preparation:

- The more prepared you are, the less anxious you will feel. Know your material inside and out.
- Prepare and organize your speech well in advance to avoid last-minute stress.

2. Practise Regularly:

- Practise your speech multiple times, both alone and in front of others. This helps you become familiar with your content and delivery.
- Rehearse in a setting similar to where you will be presenting to get comfortable with the environment.

3. Visualisation:

- Visualize yourself giving a successful speech. Imagine the audience's positive reactions and your confident delivery.

- Visualization helps build a positive mindset and reduces anxiety.

Relaxation Techniques

1. Deep Breathing:
- Practise deep breathing exercises to calm your nervous system. Inhale deeply through your nose, hold for a few seconds, and exhale slowly through your mouth.
- Deep breathing reduces physical symptoms of anxiety and helps you feel more grounded.

2. Progressive Muscle Relaxation:
- Progressive muscle relaxation involves tensing and then relaxing different muscle groups in your body.
- This technique helps release physical tension and promotes relaxation.

3. Mindfulness and Meditation:
- Practise mindfulness and meditation to stay present and focused. These techniques can help reduce overall anxiety levels.
- Spend a few minutes meditating before your speech to calm your mind and body.

Positive Thinking and Self-Talk

1. Affirmations:
- Use positive affirmations to boost your confidence. Repeat statements like "I am well-prepared and confident" or "I can handle this."
- Affirmations can reframe your mindset and reduce negative self-talk.

2. Reframing Nervousness:
- View nervousness as excitement rather than fear. The physical symptoms of both emotions are similar, so reinterpreting them can change your perspective.
- Remind yourself that a certain level of nervousness can enhance your performance by keeping you alert and focused.

3. Focus on the Message, Not Yourself:
- Shift your focus from your performance to the message you are delivering. Concentrate on the value you are providing to your audience.
- This shift in focus can reduce self-consciousness and alleviate anxiety.

Building Long-Term Confidence

Experience and Exposure

1. Start Small:
- Begin with smaller speaking opportunities to build confidence. Speak at team meetings, family gatherings, or small community events.
- Gradually take on larger audiences as you become more comfortable.

2. Seek Feedback:
- Ask for constructive feedback from trusted peers or mentors. Use their suggestions to improve your skills and build confidence.
- Positive feedback can reinforce your strengths, while constructive criticism helps you grow.

3. Record and Review:
- Record your speeches and review them to identify areas for improvement. Pay attention to both your strengths and weaknesses.
- Watching your progress over time can boost your confidence and highlight your improvement.

Developing a Positive Mindset

1. Set Realistic Goals:
- Set achievable goals for your public speaking journey. Celebrate small victories and progress rather than aiming for perfection.
- Realistic goals help you stay motivated and focused on continuous improvement.

2. Embrace Mistakes:
- Accept that mistakes are part of the learning process. Instead of fearing them, view mistakes as opportunities to learn and grow.
- Develop strategies to recover gracefully from errors during your speech.

3. Focus on Growth:
- Adopt a growth mindset, viewing challenges and feedback as opportunities for development.
- Continuously seek new learning experiences and strive to improve your skills.

Building a Support Network

1. Join Public Speaking Groups:
- Join organizations such as Toastmasters, where you can practise speaking in a supportive environment and receive constructive feedback.

- Being part of a community of like-minded individuals can provide encouragement and inspiration.

2. Find a Mentor:

- Seek out a mentor who can guide you and provide personalized advice on improving your public speaking skills.
- A mentor's experience and insights can be invaluable in building your confidence.

3. Engage with Your Audience:

- Build a rapport with your audience by engaging with them before and after your speech. Positive interactions can boost your confidence and reduce anxiety.
- Remember that your audience is generally supportive and interested in your message.

Overcoming nervousness and building confidence in public speaking is a journey that involves understanding the causes of anxiety, practising effective management techniques, and cultivating a positive mindset. By preparing thoroughly, practising relaxation techniques, and focusing on positive self-talk, you can manage nervousness effectively. Building long-term confidence requires experience, continuous learning, and a supportive network. Embrace the process, celebrate your progress, and remember that every speaking opportunity is a step toward becoming a more confident and effective speaker. With time and dedication, you can transform nervousness into a powerful tool that enhances your public speaking abilities.

This chapter provides a comprehensive guide to understanding, managing, and overcoming nervousness in public speaking. It also offers strategies for building long-term confidence.

Chapter 8
Handling Q&A Sessions

Preparing for the Q&A

Anticipating Questions

Anticipating questions is an essential part of preparing for a Q&A session. It helps you appear confident and knowledgeable, even when faced with unexpected inquiries.

1. Understand Your Audience:
- Know the demographic and background of your audience. This can give you clues about the types of questions they might ask.
- Consider their interests, concerns, and level of familiarity with your topic.

2. Review Your Content:
- Go through your presentation and identify areas that might raise questions or require further clarification.
- Think about common questions that arise around your topic and prepare answers in advance.

3. Practise with Peers:

- Conduct mock Q&A sessions with colleagues or friends. This can help you anticipate different perspectives and questions.
- Request feedback on your answers and adjust them to be clearer and more concise.

Preparing Flexible Answers

Being prepared with flexible answers means you can adapt your response to the specific context of the question.

1. Develop Key Messages:

- Identify the core messages you want to convey in your answers. These should align with the main points of your presentation.
- Practise framing your responses around these key messages, regardless of the specific question.

2. Structure Your Answers:

- Use the "PREP" formula (Point, Reason, Example, Point) to structure your answers clearly and logically.
- Start with a brief answer to the question, provide a reason or explanation, support it with an example, and then reiterate your point.

3. Be Honest and Admit When You Don't Know:
- It is okay not to have all the answers. If you do not know the answer to a question, be honest about it.
- Offer to follow up with the information later or suggest where the person can find the answer.

Conducting the Q&A Session

Managing the Flow of Questions
Effectively managing the flow of questions ensures that the Q&A session is organized and productive.

1. Set the Stage:
- At the beginning of the Q&A session, set ground rules. Explain how you will take questions (e.g., raising hands, submitting written questions).
- Let the audience know how much time is allocated for the Q&A.

2. Repeat and Clarify:
- When a question is asked, repeat it for the entire audience to hear. This ensures everyone understands the question and gives you a moment to gather your thoughts.
- If a question is unclear, ask the person to clarify it before you answer.

3. Prioritize Questions:

- Address questions that are relevant to the entire audience first. If a question is too specific or off-topic, offer to discuss it privately after the session.
- If time is running out, let the audience know you can take one or two more questions.

Engaging with the Questioner

Engaging respectfully and thoughtfully with each questioner can create a positive and interactive environment.

1. Acknowledge the Question:

- Show appreciation for the question by thanking the person. This encourages more people to participate.
- Maintain eye contact with the questioner while they are speaking and as you begin your response.

2. Stay Calm and Composed:

- Listen carefully to the entire question before responding. Take a moment to think about your answer if needed.
- Respond calmly and confidently, even if the question is challenging or critical.

3. Personalize Your Response:

- Address the questioner by name if you know it. Personalizing your response can make the interaction feel more genuine.
- Tailor your answer to the specific context or concern of the questioner.

Handling Difficult or Hostile Questions

Difficult or hostile questions can arise during Q&A sessions. Handling them with poise and professionalism is crucial.

1. Stay Professional:

- Maintain a calm and respectful demeanour, regardless of the tone of the question.
- Avoid becoming defensive or confrontational. Acknowledge the person's perspective and respond objectively.

2. Deflect and Redirect:

- If a question is off-topic or inappropriate, politely deflect and redirect the conversation back to the relevant subject.
- For example, "That's an interesting point, but let's focus on the topic at hand. I'd be happy to discuss this with you after the session."

3. Seek Common Ground:

- Find areas of agreement or common ground to build a positive connection with the questioner.
- Acknowledge valid points in their question and then provide your perspective or additional information.

Strategies for Effective Responses

Answering Clearly and Concisely

Clarity and conciseness are essential for effective communication during a Q&A session.

1. Be Direct:

- Provide a direct answer to the question first before expanding with additional details.
- Avoid unnecessary jargon or complex language that can confuse the audience.

2. Stay on Topic:

- Keep your responses focused on the question asked. If the question leads you off-topic, bring it back to the main points of your presentation.
- Summarize your answer to reinforce the key message.

3. Use Examples and Analogies:

- Use relevant examples or analogies to illustrate your points and make your answers more relatable.
- Examples can help clarify complex ideas and make your responses more engaging.

Involving the Audience

Engaging the broader audience during the Q&A can enhance the overall experience and encourage participation.

1. Encourage Participation:

- Invite questions from different sections of the audience to ensure diverse participation.
- Use phrases like "Does anyone else have a question on this topic?" to encourage more people to engage.

2. Paraphrase and Summarize:

- Paraphrase or summarize longer questions for the benefit of the audience. This ensures everyone understands the context.
- Summarizing also helps you confirm that you have understood the question correctly.

3. Connect Responses to Your Key Points:

- Link your answers back to the main points of your presentation to reinforce your message.

- This helps the audience see the relevance of the question to your overall theme.

Using Visual Aids during Q&A

Visual aids can be useful during Q&A sessions to clarify points and provide additional information.

1. Prepare Supplemental Slides:

- Have a few extra slides prepared that address potential questions or elaborate on complex points.
- These slides can provide visual support to your answers and help clarify your explanations.

2. Refer Back to Presentation Slides:

- If a question relates to something you covered earlier, refer back to the relevant slide. This can help the audience recall the information.
- Using visual aids effectively can reinforce your message and make your answers more impactful.

3. Use Props or Demonstrations:

- If appropriate, use props or live demonstrations to answer questions. This can make your response more engaging and memorable.
- Ensure any visual aids or props are easily accessible and relevant to the question.

Handling Q&A sessions effectively is a crucial skill in public speaking. By preparing for potential questions, managing the flow of the session, engaging respectfully with questioners, and providing clear, concise, and well-structured responses, you can enhance your audience's understanding and engagement. Remember to stay calm and composed, even when faced with difficult questions, and to use visual aids strategically to support your answers. With practice and preparation, you can turn the Q&A session into a valuable and interactive component of your presentation, reinforcing your message and building a positive connection with your audience.

This chapter provides comprehensive guidance on preparing for and conducting Q&A sessions, including anticipating questions, managing the flow of questions, engaging with the audience, handling difficult inquiries, and using visual aids effectively.

Chapter 9

Mastering Non-verbal Communication

Understanding Non-verbal Communication

The Importance of Non-verbal Communication

Non-verbal communication plays a crucial role in public speaking, often conveying more information than words alone. Understanding and mastering non-verbal cues can enhance your delivery and connect with your audience on a deeper level.

1. Impact on Audience Perception:

- Non-verbal cues, such as body language, facial expressions, and tone of voice, influence how your message is perceived by the audience.
- A congruent combination of verbal and non-verbal communication builds credibility, trust, and rapport with your audience.

2. Enhancing Message Clarity:

- Non-verbal cues can reinforce and clarify your verbal message. They provide additional context and emotional depth to your communication.

- Paying attention to your non-verbal communication ensures that your message is received and understood effectively.

3. Expressing Confidence and Authenticity:

- Effective non-verbal communication exudes confidence, authenticity, and authority. It helps you connect with your audience on a personal level and establish rapport.
- Mastering non-verbal cues enhances your overall presence and charisma as a speaker.

Types of Non-verbal Communication

1. Body Language:

- Body language encompasses gestures, posture, facial expressions, and eye contact. It can convey emotions, attitudes, and intentions.
- Understanding how to use body language effectively can significantly impact your ability to engage and connect with your audience.

2. Facial Expressions:

- Facial expressions are powerful communicators of emotions and attitudes. Smiling, frowning, raising eyebrows, and squinting can convey a range of feelings.

- Maintaining a warm and expressive facial demeanour can make your message more relatable and engaging.

3. Tone of Voice:
- Your tone of voice communicates emotions, emphasis, and meaning. It includes factors such as pitch, volume, pace, and intonation.
- Modulating your tone of voice can add depth and nuance to your verbal message, enhancing its impact on the audience.

Mastering Body Language

Positive Body Language Cues

1. Open Posture:
- Maintain an open and relaxed posture, with your arms uncrossed and your body facing the audience.
- Open posture signals confidence, approachability, and receptiveness to your audience.

2. Eye Contact:
- Establish and maintain eye contact with individual audience members throughout your speech. It fosters connection, engagement, and credibility.
- Distribute your gaze evenly across the audience to include everyone in the interaction.

3. Gestures:

- Use purposeful and expressive gestures to complement your verbal message. Gestures should be natural, varied, and synchronized with your speech.
- Avoid excessive or distracting gestures that may detract from your message or appear insincere.

Managing Nervous Body Language

1. Combatting Nervous Habits:

- Identify and address nervous habits such as fidgeting, pacing, or playing with objects. These behaviours can distract from your message and convey anxiety.
- Practise mindfulness and self-awareness to recognize and control nervous body language during your presentation.

2. Breathing and Relaxation Techniques:

- Practise deep breathing and relaxation techniques to manage nervous energy and reduce physical tension.
- Breathing exercises can help you stay calm and centered, allowing you to project confidence through your body language.

3. Visualization and Mental Rehearsal:

- Visualize yourself delivering your speech with calmness and confidence. Imagine maintaining poised and confident body language throughout the presentation.
- Mental rehearsal can help alleviate anxiety and reinforce positive body language cues.

Harnessing the Power of Facial Expressions

Expressive Facial Cues

1. Smiling:

- Use genuine and frequent smiles to convey warmth, friendliness, and approachability. Smiling creates a positive and welcoming atmosphere for your audience.
- Even during serious or formal presentations, incorporating appropriate smiles can humanize your message and enhance audience engagement.

2. Eye Contact and Brow Movement:

- Maintain steady and purposeful eye contact with your audience to convey sincerity, confidence, and attentiveness.
- Use eyebrow movement to express empathy, emphasis, or curiosity. Raised eyebrows can signal

interest or surprise, while furrowed eyebrows may indicate concern or focus.

3. Expressive Eyes:

- Your eyes are powerful communicators of emotions and intentions. Use eye contact, gaze direction, and pupil dilation to convey authenticity, conviction, and connection.
- Practise maintaining a warm and engaging gaze to establish rapport and connect with your audience on a personal level.

Managing Facial Expressions under Pressure

1. Maintaining Composure:

- Practise maintaining composure and control over your facial expressions, even under pressure. Project confidence and professionalism through a calm and controlled demeanour.
- Regular practice and self-awareness can help you manage facial expressions effectively, especially during challenging or high-stakes presentations.

2. Reframing Anxiety:

- Reframe anxiety as excitement or enthusiasm, channelling nervous energy into positive and expressive facial cues.

- Embrace the opportunity to connect with your audience on an emotional level, using facial expressions to convey passion, conviction, and engagement.

3. Relaxation Techniques:

- Use relaxation techniques such as deep breathing, progressive muscle relaxation, and mindfulness to alleviate tension and anxiety in facial muscles.
- Relaxed facial expressions convey confidence, authenticity, and approachability, enhancing your overall presence as a speaker.

Mastering Tone of Voice

Elements of Effective Vocal Delivery

1. Pitch Variation:

- Vary your pitch to add interest, emphasis, and emotional depth to your speech. Use a range of high and low pitches to engage your audience and convey meaning.
- Monotonous speech can be dull and disengaging, while pitch variation captures attention and maintains audience interest.

2. Volume Control:

- Modulate your volume to suit the size of the audience and the acoustics of the venue. Use a louder volume for emphasis and a softer volume for intimacy.
- Effective volume control ensures that your message is heard clearly and resonates with the audience.

3. Pace and Rhythm:

- Adjust your pace and rhythm to match the content and tone of your speech. Slow down for important points or moments of emphasis, and speed up for transitions or lighter content.
- Pauses can also be effective in adding dramatic effect and allowing the audience to process information.

4. Intonation and Inflection:

- Inflection refers to the variation in pitch and tone of voice. Use upward inflection for questions or uncertainty, and downward inflection for statements or conclusions.
- Intonation adds emotional expressiveness to your speech, conveying enthusiasm, conviction, or urgency.

5. Articulation and Clarity:

- Articulate your words clearly and enunciate consonants and vowels properly. Pay attention to pronunciation and diction to ensure that your message is conveyed accurately.
- Clear and precise articulation enhances comprehension and maintains audience engagement.

Incorporating Nonverbal Communication into Your Presentation

Integrating Body Language, Facial Expressions, and Vocal Delivery

1. Aligning Verbal and Non-verbal Cues:

- Ensure that your verbal and non-verbal communications are aligned and congruent. Your body language, facial expressions, and tone of voice should complement and reinforce your verbal message.
- Practise integrating non-verbal cues seamlessly into your presentation to enhance clarity, impact, and engagement.

2. Using Non-verbal Cues to Emphasize Key Points:

- Use non-verbal cues strategically to emphasize important points, transitions, or emotional moments in your speech. Gestures, facial expressions, and vocal delivery can amplify the significance of key messages and capture the audience's attention.

- For instance, leaning forward slightly and making eye contact can signal to the audience that an important point is being made, while a change in tone of voice can underscore the seriousness or urgency of a topic.

Creating a Connection with Your Audience

1. Establishing Rapport:
- Non-verbal communication is instrumental in building rapport and establishing a connection with your audience. Warm and inviting body language, genuine facial expressions, and expressive vocal delivery create an atmosphere of trust and engagement.
- Use non-verbal cues to demonstrate empathy, understanding, and authenticity, making your audience feel valued and respected.

2. Reading and Responding to Audience Cues:
- Pay close attention to the non-verbal cues of your audience members, such as their body language, facial expressions, and vocal responses. These cues

provide valuable feedback on their level of engagement, comprehension, and emotional state.

- Adjust your own non-verbal communication in response to audience cues to maintain connection and adapt to their needs. For example, if you notice signs of confusion, you can clarify your message or slow down your pace.

Practising Non-verbal Communication

1. Rehearsing Body Language and Facial Expressions:

- Practise your body language, facial expressions, and verbal delivery during speech rehearsals. Pay attention to the timing, intensity, and appropriateness of your non-verbal cues in relation to your message.
- Rehearsing in front of a mirror or recording yourself can help you become more aware of your non-verbal habits and refine your communication skills.

2. Seeking Feedback:

- Solicit feedback from trusted peers, mentors, or coaches on your non-verbal communication during practice sessions or actual presentations. Ask for specific observations and suggestions for improvement.
- Constructive feedback can help you identify areas of strength and areas that need further development,

allowing you to refine your non-verbal communication skills effectively.

Developing Self-Awareness

1. Reflecting on Non-verbal Communication:
- Take time to reflect on your own non-verbal communication patterns, habits, and tendencies. Consider how your body language, facial expressions, and vocal delivery contribute to your overall communication style and impact.
- Identify both strengths and areas for improvement, and set specific goals for enhancing your non-verbal communication skills in future presentations.

2. Practising Mindfulness:
- Practise mindfulness techniques to increase your self-awareness and control over your non-verbal communication. Be present and attentive to your body language, facial expressions, and vocal tone during presentations.
- Mindfulness can help you regulate your non-verbal cues, manage nervousness, and maintain focus and composure, leading to more effective communication and connection with your audience.

Mastering non-verbal communication is essential for becoming a confident and impactful public speaker. By understanding the importance of non-verbal cues, mastering body language, facial expressions, and vocal delivery, and incorporating non-verbal communication into your presentation, you can enhance your ability to connect with your audience, convey your message with clarity and authenticity, and create a memorable and engaging speaking experience. With practice, self-awareness, and mindful attention to your non-verbal communication, you can elevate your public speaking skills and make a lasting impression on your audience.

This chapter provides comprehensive guidance on understanding, mastering, and incorporating non-verbal communication into your presentations, including body language, facial expressions, tone of voice, and strategies for creating a connection with your audience.

Chapter 10

Using Visual Aids Effectively

Understanding the Role of Visual Aids

The Importance of Visual Aids in Presentations

Visual aids are powerful tools that complement verbal communication, enhance audience understanding, and increase retention of key information. Understanding how to use visual aids effectively can significantly improve the impact and effectiveness of your presentations.

1. Enhancing Comprehension:

- Visual aids help illustrate complex concepts, data, and ideas in a clear and accessible manner.
- They provide visual reinforcement and clarification, making it easier for the audience to grasp and retain information presented verbally.

2. Increasing Engagement:

- Visual aids capture the audience's attention and maintain their interest throughout the presentation.

- Well-designed and engaging visual elements add variety to the presentation, preventing monotony and boredom.

3. Supporting Persuasion:

- Visual aids can be powerful tools for persuasion, influencing the audience's opinions, attitudes, and behaviours.
- They provide visual evidence, examples, and arguments to support your key points and reinforce the persuasive impact of your message.

Types of Visual Aids

Choosing the Right Visual Aid for Your Presentation
Selecting the appropriate visual aid depends on the content of your presentation, the preferences of your audience, and the objectives you aim to achieve. Here are some common types of visual aids and their applications:

1. Presentation Slides:

- Presentation slides are widely used visual aids that consist of text, images, graphs, charts, and multimedia elements.
- They provide a structured framework for organizing and delivering your presentation, guiding the audience through key points and supporting information.

- Presentation slides are effective for illustrating complex ideas, highlighting important data, and enhancing the overall visual appeal of your presentation.

2. Graphs and Charts:

- Graphs and charts are visual representations of data that help convey numerical information in a concise and easily understandable format.
- They include bar graphs, line graphs, pie charts, histograms, and scatter plots, among others.
- Graphs and charts are useful for illustrating trends, comparisons, patterns, and relationships within the data, making complex information more accessible and meaningful to the audience.

3. Diagrams and Models:

- Diagrams and models are visual representations that depict processes, structures, systems, or relationships.
- They include flowcharts, organizational charts, mind maps, Venn diagrams, and 3D models, among others.
- Diagrams and models are effective for explaining complex concepts, illustrating sequential processes, and visualizing abstract ideas, enhancing audience understanding and engagement.

4. Images and Illustrations:

- Images and illustrations are visual elements that enhance the aesthetic appeal and visual impact of your presentation.
- They include photographs, illustrations, diagrams, icons, and symbols.
- Images and illustrations are powerful tools for capturing the audience's attention, evoking emotions, and adding context and relevance to your message.

5. Videos and Multimedia:

- Videos and multimedia elements such as audio clips, animations, and interactive presentations can enrich your presentation and create a dynamic and engaging experience for the audience.
- They provide opportunities for storytelling, demonstrations, testimonials, and real-life examples that enhance the audience's understanding and retention of key concepts.

Designing Effective Visual Aids

Principles of Visual Aid Design

Creating effective visual aids requires careful planning, design, and execution to ensure clarity, coherence, and visual appeal. Here are some key principles to consider:

1. Simplicity:

- Keep visual aids simple and uncluttered to avoid overwhelming the audience with excessive information.
- Use clear and concise language, minimal text, and simple graphics to convey your message effectively.

2. Consistency:

- Maintain consistency in design elements such as colour schemes, fonts, and formatting throughout your visual aids.
- Consistency helps create a cohesive, professional-looking presentation that is visually appealing and easy to follow.

3. Clarity:

- Ensure that visual aids are easy to read, understand, and interpret by using appropriate font sizes, colours, and styles.
- Use high-quality images and graphics that are relevant to your content and convey the intended message clearly.

4. Relevance:

- Select visual aids that are relevant to your content and directly support your key points and arguments.

- Avoid using visual elements that are distracting or tangential to the main focus of your presentation.

5. Accessibility:
- Design visual aids with accessibility in mind to ensure that all audience members can easily perceive and interpret the information presented.
- Consider factors such as colour contrast, text size, and alternative formats for individuals with visual or cognitive impairments.

Incorporating Visual Aids into Your Presentation

Strategies for Seamless Integration

Integrating visual aids effectively into your presentation involves careful planning, rehearsal, and coordination to ensure that they enhance rather than detract from your message. Here are some strategies for seamless integration:

1. Introduction and Context:
- Introduce each visual aid clearly and provide context for its relevance to the topic or point you are addressing.
- Explain the purpose of the visual aid and how it contributes to the overall understanding and impact of your presentation.

2. Strategic Placement:

- Place visual aids strategically within your presentation to coincide with the corresponding verbal content.
- Use visual aids to illustrate key points, highlight important data, and reinforce your main arguments at relevant points throughout the presentation.

3. Timing and Pace:

- Control the timing and pace of your presentation to ensure that visual aids are displayed at the appropriate moments and for the appropriate durations.
- Avoid overwhelming the audience with too many visual aids or displaying them for too long, which can distract from your verbal message.

4. Engagement and Interaction:

- Encourage audience engagement and interaction with visual aids by inviting questions, eliciting feedback, and facilitating discussions.
- Use visual aids as prompts for audience participation, prompting thought-provoking questions, or encouraging reflection on key concepts.

Handling Technical Challenges

Troubleshooting and Contingency Planning

Despite careful preparation, technical challenges may arise when using visual aids during presentations. Being prepared to handle such challenges effectively can help minimize disruptions and maintain the flow of your presentation. Here are some common technical challenges and strategies for addressing them:

1. Equipment Malfunctions:

- Have backup equipment and contingency plans in place in case of technical malfunctions such as projector failure, screen freeze, or audio issues.
- Familiarize yourself with the operation of the equipment and troubleshooting procedures to resolve technical issues quickly and efficiently.

2. File Compatibility Issues:

- Ensure that your visual aid files are compatible with the presentation software and hardware being used.
- Convert files to appropriate formats and test compatibility in advance to avoid unexpected formatting or display errors during the presentation.

3. Internet Connectivity Problems:

- If your presentation relies on online content or multimedia elements, ensure that you have a reliable internet connection and backup options available.
- Download and save online content locally to your device as a backup in case of internet connectivity issues.

4. Backup Plans:

- Develop backup plans and alternative strategies for delivering your presentation in the event of unforeseen technical challenges.
- Consider offline presentation options, printed hand-outs, or verbal explanations as alternatives to visual aids if necessary.

Using visual aids effectively is an essential skill for delivering engaging, informative, and impactful presentations. By understanding the role of visual aids, choosing the right types of visual aids for your content, designing them effectively, and incorporating them seamlessly into your presentation, you can enhance audience comprehension, engagement, and retention of key information. Additionally, being prepared to handle technical challenges ensures that your presentation runs smoothly and maintains its impact even in the face of unexpected obstacles.

This chapter provides comprehensive guidance on understanding, designing, incorporating, and troubleshooting visual aids in presentations, including the importance of visual aids, types of visual aids, principles of visual aid design, strategies for integration, and handling technical challenges.

Chapter 11

Engaging Your Audience

Understanding Audience Engagement

The Importance of Audience Engagement in Presentations

Audience engagement is a critical aspect of effective public speaking, as it allows speakers to connect with their audience, maintain interest, and deliver a memorable and impactful presentation. Understanding how to engage your audience can significantly enhance the success of your presentations.

1. Fostering Active Participation:

- Audience engagement encourages active participation and interaction, transforming presentations into dynamic and two-way communication experiences.
- Engaged audiences are more attentive, receptive, and responsive to the speaker's message, leading to increased comprehension and retention of key information.

2. Building Connection and Rapport:
- Engaging your audience helps build a connection and rapport, creating a positive and supportive atmosphere for communication and learning.
- A connected audience is more likely to relate to the speaker, empathize with their message, and be influenced by their ideas and arguments.

3. Enhancing Learning and Retention:
- Engaged audiences are more likely to learn, retain, and apply the information presented during a presentation.
- Interactive and participatory presentations stimulate cognitive processes such as attention, memory, and critical thinking, leading to deeper understanding and long-term retention of key concepts.

Strategies for Audience Engagement

Effective Techniques for Engaging Your Audience

Engaging your audience requires a combination of effective communication strategies, interactive techniques, and audience-centered approaches. Here are some strategies for engaging your audience and keeping them actively involved throughout your presentation:

1. Start with a Strong Opening:

- Capture the audience's attention and interest from the very beginning with a strong and compelling opening.
- Use attention-grabbing techniques such as storytelling, humour, provocative questions, startling facts, or thought-provoking quotes to pique curiosity and create a memorable impression.

2. Know Your Audience:

- Tailor your presentation to the interests, needs, and preferences of your audience to ensure relevance and resonance.
- Conduct audience analysis and research to understand their demographics, background, knowledge level, and expectations, and adapt your content and delivery accordingly.

3. Interactive Polls and Surveys:

- Incorporate interactive polls, surveys, or audience response systems into your presentation to encourage active participation and gather feedback.
- Polls and surveys can be used to gauge audience opinions, preferences, and prior knowledge, fostering engagement and dialogue throughout the presentation.

4. Group Activities and Discussions:

- Divide the audience into small groups or pairs and facilitate interactive activities, discussions, or brainstorming sessions related to the presentation topic.
- Group activities promote collaboration, engagement, and peer learning, allowing participants to actively explore and apply key concepts in a supportive and interactive environment.

5. Q&A Sessions:

- Allocate time for questions and answers throughout the presentation to encourage audience interaction and address any queries or concerns.
- Encourage audience members to ask questions, share their perspectives, and participate in meaningful dialogue, fostering engagement and active involvement in the presentation.

6. Incorporate Multimedia and Visual Aids:

- Use multimedia elements, visual aids, and interactive technologies such as videos, images, animations, and live demonstrations to enhance the visual appeal and interactivity of your presentation.
- Multimedia and visual aids captivate the audience's attention, illustrate key points, and stimulate

multiple senses, making the presentation more engaging and memorable.

Creating Interactive Presentations

Designing Presentations for Maximum Engagement

Designing interactive presentations involves structuring content, incorporating interactive elements, and facilitating audience participation to create a dynamic and engaging presentation experience. Here's how to create interactive presentations that captivate and involve your audience:

1. Outline Clear Objectives:
- Clearly define the objectives and goals of your presentation, as well as the desired outcomes for audience engagement and participation.
- Set specific objectives for each interactive element or activity, ensuring that they align with the overall purpose and content of the presentation.

2. Plan Interactive Segments:
- Identify key points, transitions, or sections within your presentation where interactive elements or activities can be integrated seamlessly.
- Plan interactive segments such as polls, quizzes, discussions, or group activities to coincide with relevant topics, allowing for meaningful

engagement and interaction throughout the presentation.

3. Engage the Audience Early and Often:

- Begin engaging your audience from the outset of your presentation and continue to involve them at regular intervals throughout the session.
- Incorporate interactive elements, questions, or activities into the opening, body, and conclusion of your presentation to maintain momentum and sustain audience engagement from start to finish.

4. Encourage Active Participation:

- Encourage active participation by providing clear instructions, prompts, and opportunities for audience members to contribute, share their thoughts, and interact with the content.
- Create a supportive and inclusive environment where all audience members feel comfortable and empowered to participate actively in the presentation.

5. Facilitate Meaningful Discussions:

- Facilitate discussions, debates, or brainstorming sessions that encourage audience members to critically analyze, discuss, and apply key concepts presented during the presentation.

- Pose open-ended questions, present case studies, or invite audience members to share their own experiences and perspectives, fostering meaningful dialogue and exploration of the topic.

6. Conclude with Reflection and Call to Action:

- Conclude your presentation with a reflective summary of key insights, takeaways, and action points discussed during the session.
- Encourage audience members to reflect on what they have learned, identify actionable steps, and commit to applying the knowledge gained from the presentation in their own lives or work contexts.

Overcoming Challenges in Audience Engagement

Strategies for Addressing Common Challenges

While engaging an audience is essential for successful presentations, speakers may encounter various challenges that can impede audience participation and interaction. Here are some common challenges and strategies for overcoming them:

1. Lack of Interest or Attention:

- Capture the audience's interest and attention from the outset with a compelling opening that relates to their interests, needs, or concerns.

- Use engaging storytelling, visuals, or interactive elements to maintain interest and sustain attention throughout the presentation.

2. Audience Disengagement or Distractions:

- Monitor audience engagement and adjust your presentation style, content, or delivery to re-engage disengaged or distracted audience members.
- Incorporate interactive elements, group activities, or audience participation opportunities to rekindle interest and involvement in the presentation.

3. Technical Issues or Logistics:

- Prepare in advance for potential technical issues or logistical challenges that may arise during the presentation.
- Conduct thorough equipment checks, have backup plans in place, and ensure that all necessary resources and materials are readily accessible and functioning properly.

4. Overcoming Language or Cultural Barriers:

- Tailor your presentation to accommodate diverse language and cultural backgrounds within the audience.
- Use simple and clear language, avoid jargon or technical terms, and provide translations or

explanations as needed to ensure universal understanding and inclusivity.

Engaging your audience is essential for delivering impactful and memorable presentations that captivate, inform, and inspire. By understanding the importance of audience engagement, implementing effective engagement strategies, creating interactive presentations, and overcoming common challenges, you can create a dynamic and interactive presentation experience that resonates with your audience and achieves your communication goals.

This chapter provides comprehensive guidance on understanding the importance of audience engagement, implementing effective strategies for engaging your audience, creating interactive presentations, and overcoming common challenges in audience engagement during presentations.

Chapter 12

Handling Q&A Sessions Effectively

Understanding the Role of Q&A Sessions

The Importance of Q&A Sessions in Presentations

Question and Answer (Q&A) sessions are a valuable component of presentations that allow speakers to engage with their audience, address inquiries, and clarify key points. Understanding how to handle Q&A sessions effectively is essential for fostering dialogue, building rapport, and reinforcing the impact of your presentation.

1. Fostering Engagement and Interaction:

- Q&A sessions provide an opportunity for audience members to actively participate in the presentation, ask questions, and contribute to the discussion.
- Engaging in dialogue with the audience fosters interaction, promotes a sense of inclusivity, and enhances overall engagement with the presentation.

2. Clarifying Key Points and Addressing Concerns:

- Q&A sessions enable speakers to clarify complex concepts, elaborate on key points, and address any concerns or uncertainties raised by the audience.
- Responding to audience questions in real time allows speakers to provide additional context, examples, and explanations, enhancing audience comprehension and retention of the material presented.

3. Building Credibility and Trust:

- Effective handling of Q&A sessions demonstrates the speaker's expertise, knowledge, and preparedness, building credibility and trust with the audience.
- Openly engaging with audience inquiries and addressing them with confidence and clarity reinforces the speaker's authority and authenticity, strengthening the connection with the audience.

Strategies for Handling Q&A Sessions

Effective Techniques for Managing Q&A Sessions

Successfully managing Q&A sessions requires preparation, active listening, and effective communication skills. Here are some strategies for handling Q&A sessions effectively and maximizing their impact:

1. Prepare for Potential Questions:

- Anticipate potential questions that the audience may ask based on the content of your presentation, the topic, and the interests of the audience.
- Review your presentation materials, identify key points, and prepare concise and thoughtful responses to commonly asked questions in advance.

2. Active Listening:

- Listen attentively to each question posed by the audience, demonstrating respect and interest in their inquiries.
- Maintain eye contact with the individual asking the question, nodding or acknowledging their question to signal that you are actively listening and ready to respond.

3. Repeat or Paraphrase Questions:

- Repeat or paraphrase each question before providing your response to ensure clarity and understanding, especially for larger audiences or in noisy environments.
- Rephrasing the question also allows you to confirm your understanding of the inquiry and provides an opportunity to reframe the question if necessary.

4. Be Concise and Clear in Your Responses:

- Provide concise and clear responses to audience questions, focusing on addressing the core of the inquiry without unnecessary elaboration.
- Use simple and accessible language, avoid technical jargon or complex terminology, and provide concrete examples or illustrations to enhance understanding.

5. Acknowledge Limitations and Offer to Follow Up:

- If you encounter a question to which you do not know the answer, acknowledge the limitation and offer to follow up with additional information after the presentation.
- Express gratitude for the question and assure the audience member that you will provide a comprehensive response or direct them to additional resources as needed.

6. Encourage Audience Participation:

- Foster audience participation and engagement by encouraging questions, comments, and feedback throughout the Q&A session.
- Create a welcoming and supportive environment where audience members feel comfortable expressing their thoughts, sharing their perspectives, and actively participating in the discussion.

Managing Challenging Questions

Strategies for Addressing Difficult Inquiries

Handling challenging or unexpected questions during Q&A sessions requires composure, preparation, and tactful communication. Here are some strategies for addressing challenging questions effectively and maintaining control of the Q&A session:

1. Remain Calm and Composed:

- Maintain a calm and composed demeanour when faced with challenging or confrontational questions, avoiding defensive or confrontational responses.
- Take a moment to pause, collect your thoughts, and formulate a composed and respectful response to the inquiry.

2. Acknowledge and Validate the Question:

- Acknowledge the validity and importance of the question, even if it is challenging or critical in nature.
- Express appreciation for the question and demonstrate openness to addressing concerns or perspectives that may differ from your own.

3. Redirect to Key Points:

- Redirect the focus of the response to key points or messages from your presentation that are relevant to the question.
- Use the opportunity to reinforce key messages, highlight supporting evidence, or provide additional context that aligns with the theme of your presentation.

4. Maintain Control and Stay on Topic:

- Maintain control of the Q&A session and steer the discussion back to the main topics and objectives of your presentation.
- Politely but firmly redirect the conversation if it veers off-topic or becomes overly contentious, emphasizing the importance of staying focused on the presentation content.

5. Offer Balanced and Constructive Responses:

- Provide balanced and constructive responses to challenging questions, addressing both positive and negative aspects of the inquiry.
- Offer thoughtful insights, practical solutions, or alternative perspectives that demonstrate your ability to navigate complex issues and engage in constructive dialogue.

Enhancing Audience Interaction

Promoting Engagement and Dialogue

Promoting audience interaction and dialogue during Q&A sessions contributes to a dynamic and engaging presentation experience. Here are some strategies for enhancing audience interaction and fostering meaningful dialogue during Q&A sessions:

1. Encourage Diverse Perspectives:

- Encourage audience members to share diverse perspectives, insights, and experiences related to the presentation topic.
- Create an inclusive and open-minded environment where all viewpoints are respected and valued, fostering constructive dialogue and mutual learning.

2. Facilitate Peer-to-Peer Discussions:

- Facilitate peer-to-peer discussions and exchanges by inviting audience members to respond to each other's questions, share relevant examples, or offer alternative viewpoints.
- Encourage active listening, empathy, and respectful communication among audience members, promoting collaborative learning and knowledge sharing.

3. Use Group Activities or Breakout Sessions:

- Divide the audience into small groups or pairs and facilitate group activities, discussions, or brainstorming sessions related to the presentation topic.
- Group activities promote collaboration, engagement, and peer learning, allowing participants to actively explore and apply key concepts in a supportive and interactive environment.

Effectively managing Q&A sessions is an essential skill for public speakers, as it enables them to engage with their audience, address inquiries, and reinforce key messages presented during the presentation. By understanding the role of Q&A sessions, implementing effective strategies for handling questions, managing challenging inquiries, and promoting audience interaction, speakers can create a dynamic and interactive presentation experience that resonates with their audience and achieves their communication goals.

This chapter provides comprehensive guidance on understanding the role of Q&A sessions in presentations, implementing effective strategies for managing Q&A sessions, addressing challenging questions, and promoting audience interaction and dialogue.

Conclusion

As you reach the conclusion of this comprehensive guide to public speaking, it is essential to reflect on the valuable insights, strategies, and techniques you have learned to enhance your speaking skills and captivate your audience. Throughout this book, we have explored every aspect of public speaking, from the initial preparation to the delivery and engagement with your audience.

As you continue your public speaking journey, remember that mastering the art of public speaking is an ongoing process of growth, learning, and refinement. By applying the principles, techniques, and strategies outlined in this book and embracing opportunities for practice and feedback, you will continue to develop and strengthen your speaking skills over time.

Now that you have acquired a comprehensive understanding of public speaking and a diverse repertoire of speaking techniques and strategies, it is time to put your knowledge into action. Commit to applying what you have learned in real-world speaking engagements, whether in professional, academic, or personal settings. Remember that every speaking opportunity is a chance to refine your skills, connect with your audience, and make a meaningful impact with your message.

Finally, I want to express my gratitude for accompanying me on this journey through the art of public speaking. Your dedication to improving your speaking skills is commendable, and I am confident that you will continue to inspire and influence others with your newfound confidence, clarity, and authenticity as a speaker. Remember that your voice has the power to inform, persuade, and inspire change in the world around you. Keep speaking up, sharing your ideas, and making a difference in the lives of others.

As you embark on the next phase of your public speaking journey, I wish you continued success, growth, and fulfilment as a confident and impactful speaker. May your presentations inspire, engage, and leave a lasting impression on your audience, making a positive difference in the world one speech at a time.

This conclusion encapsulates the key learnings and encourages continuous growth and application of the skills acquired throughout the book.